Original title:
Shadows of the Shagbark

Copyright © 2025 Creative Arts Management OÜ
All rights reserved.

Author: Aurora Sinclair
ISBN HARDBACK: 978-1-80567-259-3
ISBN PAPERBACK: 978-1-80567-558-7

Memory Embedded in Roots

In the dim where laughter hides,
Squirrels play their little pranks.
Leaves giggle in the gentle breeze,
While bees throw tiny dance flanks.

A turtle wearing ten hats,
Strolls through grass in such delight.
Rabbits hop with goofy hats,
Underneath the moonlight bright.

The Pulse of a Hidden World

A beetle plays a wild drum,
While worms conduct a band of haste.
Frogs croak in a comic hum,
In a garden, time's too waste.

The snails hold a slow race,
While crickets try to sing along.
Each face in nature's embrace,
Cheers for every silly song.

Between Halos and Gnarled Roots

Old branches gossip with the wind,
Whispering tales of the past.
With playful roots that twist and bend,
Every secret's meant to last.

A nut falls with a comical thud,
The chipmunks scatter in surprise.
Mice share jokes while chewing cud,
In nature's world, laughter flies.

The Tangle of Nature's Dreams

In the maze of wild vine curls,
Frogs wear hats made of dear moss.
Dancing leaves give silly twirls,
As ponds mirror laughter's gloss.

A fox spins tales of old fright,
While owls roll their big round eyes.
Nature's fun; a true delight,
Where every creature climaxes lies.

The Groove of Footsteps Past

In the park, we dance around,
With two left feet, we hit the ground.
A squirrel laughs, a bird does cheer,
As we trip over roots, oh dear!

Old paths where we used to run,
Now just stories, all in fun.
With every slip and playful fall,
The echoes of laughter, we recall.

Nature's Loom: A Tangle of Tales

A spider spins a sticky thread,
To catch the tales our feet have led.
The trees gossip about our ways,
As we frolic in their sunny rays.

Branches nodding, leaves all sway,
While we make silly sounds and play.
The woods have seen our goofy dance,
And they're here for our next chance!

Chronicles Written in Bark

Each tree stands tall, its scars ablaze,
With stories of our clumsy phase.
We carved our names, then slipped and fell,
Now criminals of nature, oh well!

The woods laugh loud, the critters tease,
As branches tickle through the breeze.
In this bark, our tales disguise,
Of goofy moves and wild surprise!

Moonlit Musings Amongst Trees

Under the moon, we trip and slide,
The shadows dance, they try to hide.
With giggles echoing in the night,
We can't stop laughing, what a sight!

A raccoon joins, with mischief bright,
We waddle and tumble in delight.
In this moonlit game, we break free,
Of worries and woes, just wild spree!

Where the Light Meets the Moss

In the forest, where squirrels peek,
Moss grows thick, a comfy cheek.
Fungi dance, in colors bright,
Who's the boss? The mushrooms might!

A raccoon winks with a sly smile,
Wearing masks, he walks in style.
Algae giggles in a stream,
Together, they form quite the team!

A chipmunk trips on a leafy trail,
With acorn friends, he tells a tale.
The sun's rays poke through the trees,
Nature's jest, a playful tease!

Where laughter blends with hues of green,
Life's a jest, you know what I mean?
In the underbrush, a funny sight,
Light meets moss in pure delight!

Twilight's Quilt of Nature

As dusk weaves in its cozy thread,
Creatures stir from dream-based beds.
Fireflies twinkle, a disco show,
Frogs croak groovy tunes below!

A wise old owl hoots a joke,
On a branch, a tired crow awoke.
"Why did the chicken cross the path?"
"Chasing shadows, doing the math!"

Bats zip past in a playful flight,
Chasing stars, just out of sight.
Crickets chirp their nightly song,
In nature's tale, we all belong!

When twilight wraps the world in cheer,
Whispers linger, bright and clear.
With nature's quilt, we softly sway,
Laughing through the end of day!

The Solace of Twisted Limbs

Beneath a tree with limbs askew,
Squirrels plot mischief, just a few.
A branch bends low for a squirrel's seat,
A sticky paw, a tasty treat!

Twisted trunks with faces grim,
Whisper secrets on a whim.
Laughter echoes from silent wood,
"Life is wacky! Isn't it good?"

Bees buzz by with a mission clear,
Join the dance, let's spread some cheer!
In a patch of light, shadows glide,
Nature's chuckle, we can't hide!

With crooked roots, we find our glee,
In every nook, a mystery.
Two owls wink, a knowing jest,
In shady nooks, we find our rest!

Embrace of the Roaming Wind

The wind does laugh, a cheeky breeze,
Tugging hats, oh what a tease!
Whirling leaves in a spin so neat,
Nature's dance, what a wild beat!

A butterfly flutters with flair,
Scoffing clouds without a care.
"Catch me if you can!" it shouts,
Playful nature leaves no doubts!

Raccoons tumble, chasing their tail,
While dandelions send seeds to sail.
In each gust, a chuckle flies,
The world spins round, under the skies!

With gentle whispers, the winds proclaim,
Life's a game, it's never tame.
Through chaos found in a playful stride,
We embrace the fun, and laugh with pride!

The Mystic Hum of Nature's Heart

In the woods, a whisper sings,
Critters chat about strange things.
Squirrels juggle acorns round,
While owls wear capes and strut the ground.

Bears partake in tea so fine,
Discussing which tree has the best wine.
Frogs croak jokes with a funky beat,
While raccoons dance on furry feet.

The sun peeks in, all golden and bright,
Casting silliness in morning light.
Around the bend, the bushes shake,
With a hare that bakes a pie with cake.

Each leaf whispers tales from afar,
Of the time a deer played on a guitar.
Nature's heart beats a playful drum,
Inviting us all to join the fun.

Beneath the Graying Sun

Under the sun where grays collide,
An old toad jumps with humorous pride.
He claims to be the king of the mud,
While snails line up to join his club.

A crow struts in with a silly caw,
Dressed in feathers that spark a raw.
Squirrels giggle from their leafy perch,
As they witness this bizarre church.

The wind plays tricks, tugs at each branch,
As flowers sway in a clumsy dance.
Bees buzz laughter, quite thrilled to roam,
A parade of colors finds its home.

Laughter ripples through the bright haze,
As sunlight casts its quirky rays.
Amidst the gloom, joy sprouts and grows,
In a world where even the mushy glows.

The Interplay of Gloom and Glory

A gloomy crow flew through the mist,
Tripped on a twig, he couldn't resist.
With flapping wings and a comical squawk,
He cursed the day, taking to the walk.

But glory shines on a fox with flair,
Dancing around without a care.
She leaps through ferns, a joyous sprite,
Making the woods feel extra bright.

With a plop, a raccoon falls in a stream,
While fish giggle, a slippery dream.
Laughter echoes as he shakes it dry,
Underneath trees that nod and sigh.

Though shadows may loom, joy's in the air,
Every creature finds ways to share.
Gloom and glory tango and spin,
In a woodland tale where all can win.

Sighs of the Forgotten Forest

In the forgotten woods, a cheeky breeze,
Tells tales of trees who just want to tease.
Old roots gossip, sharing the news,
Of a turtle who tried on a pair of shoes.

The grumpy oak grumbles, 'I need a day off,'
As acorns tumble down with a scoff.
Hedgehogs chuckle, snorting with glee,
At the sight of a squirrel stuck in a tree.

Beneath tales of woe and whimsical plight,
Fungi wear hats, oh what a sight!
Jellyfish dance through the dappled glade,
Dreaming of jelly that somehow stayed.

Every sigh of the old woods, it seems,
Hides laughter and nonsense in secret dreams.
Nature's punchlines float in the air,
Whispering jokes for those who dare.

Under the Cloak of Ageing Trees

Beneath the limbs that creak and sway,
Old branches chuckle, come what may.
They tell the tales of years gone by,
Of squirrels plotting mischief up high.

The leaves are laughing, green and bright,
As daisies dance in the dappled light.
With every gust, a giggle grows,
While acorns drop with cheeky prose.

Mossy carpets cushion their feet,
An ancient stage for a leafy feat.
The roots have stories, so divine,
Of beetles dating back in time.

Under the cloak, oh what a scene,
Nature's stand-up, rich and keen.
With every rustle, every tease,
Life waits patiently with a breeze.

Whispers of the Wind in Foliage

The whispers rustle through the leaves,
Bringing giggles, like a tease.
The branches sway in cheerful jest,
As if they're hosting nature's fest.

A breeze that tickles bark and stem,
Joking with the flowers' hem.
In patches bright, the colors bloom,
While playful breezes sweep the gloom.

The ferns are swaying to the song,
Of winds that whirl both bold and strong.
They gossip softly, share a laugh,
As frogs take turns to show their path.

With every gust, a secret shared,
Old trees nod gently, showing they cared.
The wind, a friend, so full of zest,
Blows life into their leafy quest.

The Memory of Tree-Laden Trails

Along the paths where branches bend,
Old tales echo, never end.
The trunks hold laughter, secrets deep,
In every hollow, memories creep.

Footsteps shuffle through the brush,
While timid critters dart and rush.
The way unwinds with every twist,
It's hard to know what you might miss.

Each twist of bark and gnarled root,
Seems to giggle and salute.
Nature's stage, with every mile,
Tripping lightly, with a smile.

Oh, what a journey, wild and free,
Where whispers giggle beneath the tree.
In every nook, something to find,
Trails full of fun, leaving worries behind.

Flickers of Light in Darkened Corners

In corners dark where critters hide,
Flickers happen, like giggling tide.
Fireflies dance with cheeky grace,
   Illuminating nature's embrace.

The shadows play a playful trick,
As beetles race and crickets click.
With every hum, a whisper lingers,
   Life's little comedy, on fingers.

Old roots entwined like laughter's flow,
   Each twist a jest, each turn, a show.
The darkened nooks of woodland's heart,
   Are bursting full of nature's art.

In light's flickers, humor sows,
A symphony where joy just grows.
In every shadow, a story shines,
   In hidden corners, the fun aligns.

The Beneath of Nature's Canvas

In the dark, critters joke,
Squirrels plotting with a poke.
Mice are brazen, dance with glee,
While rabbits hop like they're on a spree.

Leaves are giggling in the breeze,
Tickling branches with such ease.
Whispers echo, branches sway,
Nature's jesters at a play.

Underfoot, the earthworms grin,
As the dandelions spin and spin.
Fungi claps a spongy cheer,
While the wildflowers shed a tear.

Nature's laughter fills the wood,
In this realm where life is good.
So come and join this lively scene,
With silly sights—a vibrant green.

Where Roots and Whispers Intertwine

Roots are tangled, secrets kept,
Where mischievous fairies leapt.
Toadstools giggle, paths unclear,
As shadows tangle without fear.

Beneath the trees, a ruckus swells,
With whispers shared in leafy spells.
Bumblebees don hats of winks,
Dancing as the sunlight blinks.

The brook chuckles, ripples play,
Fish make faces, splashing spray.
All while the owls hoot with glee,
In this circus of giddy glee.

Nature's mischief runs amok,
While wise old oaks stay in shock.
Join the fun, don't be shy,
In this realm where giggles fly.

Chronicles of the Whispering Woods

Deep in the green, the trees conspire,
To craft tales that never tire.
With giggles bubbling from their bark,
And mischief lurking in the dark.

Barking dogs might need a snack,
But squirrels plot to steal it back.
With acorns tossed like juggling balls,
And echoes of their playful calls.

Throughout the thicket, laughter zips,
As mice waltz on their tiny tips.
Grasshoppers croon in a jazzy tone,
While mushrooms boast they're not alone.

In this whimsical, wild parade,
Every critter joins the charade.
So grab a leaf and sway along,
In this forest's merry song.

Nightfall Amongst the Ancient Boughs

As dusk descends, the owls all grin,
In twilight's glow, the fun begins.
Fireflies twirl in winking lights,
In a dance of laughter and silly sights.

Crickets chirp their nightly tune,
While stars giggle, peeking soon.
Branches sway like they're in cheer,
For the quirks that night will steer.

Barks of trees wear a grin so wide,
As raccoons venture with nothing to hide.
The moon chuckles, casting glow,
On this party of nature's show.

When night is young and spirits bright,
Join the woods for this delight.
In every creak, in every rustle,
Lies the heart of nature's hustle.

Boughs That Hide the Night

In a tangle of limbs, a raccoon sneaks,
With a stash of snacks, he plays hide and seek.
He chuckles aloud, thinking it grand,
While the owl rolls his eyes, with plans unplanned.

Above them, the stars, so twinkling bright,
Wonder if raccoons are all just alright.
They dance on the breeze, so full of glee,
While shadows plot pranks, oh, can't you see!

Echoing Through the Hollow Trees

A squirrel debates, 'Should I take that leap?'
While the branches below giggle, cozy and deep.
They whisper for him to let out a squeak,
But gravity's joke makes his heart feel weak.

Once on the ground, with a thud, oh dear!
The laughter erupts, echoing near.
'Next time,' he vows, 'I'll plan my detail!'
But the trees just sway, their laughter won't fail.

The Silent Watchers: A Grove's Tale

The trees stand tall, like guards of the wood,
With hats made of leaves, they play like they should.
They mimic the songs of the birds that they hear,
While critters roll by, grinning ear to ear.

A deer with a bowtie attends the whole show,
While the grass tickles toes, as breezes blow.
The drama unfolds, friendships reborn,
In a world where the leaves lean and giggle at dawn.

Fragments of Forgotten Roofs

Beneath the old roofs, a treasure trove lies,
A cap full of nuts and some discarded fries.
The raccoons swap tales of the nights spent in dream,
While the moon beams down—oh, it's quite the team!

A jester of sorts, a crow steals the scene,
With a quip or two that keeps spirits keen.
The rooftops may crumble, but laughter won't fade,
In a world where folly and friendship are made.

The Whisper of Old Growth

Beneath the branches, squirrels sway,
A chorus of creaks as they play.
Old trunks chuckle, roots intertwine,
Nature's jesters, with humor divine.

Laughter rustles through the leaves,
A dance of branches, as one believes.
The wisdom of ages, but still so spry,
Indeed, who knew trees could be so sly!

Murmurs Among the Colonies of Green

In the thicket, secrets thrive,
Whispering gently, the critters contrive.
A rabbit quips, 'That mushroom's fine!'
While a wise owl hoots, 'Not this time!'

A raccoon spins tales of midnight feasts,
While the possum plays dead, as he usually feasts.
Laughter ensues from the mossy floor,
'Though the humor's old, we can't get bored!'

In the Grip of Nature's Clutch

The vines are laughing, tangled and tight,
'You'll never escape, oh what a sight!'
A bear's got the munchies; he's raiding a hive,
'If honey's thegoal, I'll party alive!'

Frogs trade puns near the shimmering brook,
Each ripple echoes, like pages in a book.
'What's green and hops? This joke's a clutch!'
The whole forest cackles, enjoying the touch!

Lanterns in the Gloomy Grove

Fireflies flicker, like lights in a dance,
They giggle and twirl in a twinkling prance.
'Who turned off the stars?' a fox peers around,
'Oh wait, I forgot! They live on the ground!'

The trees in their robes, with mossy old capes,
Share ticklish tales of their leafy escapes.
Beneath every lantern, a fun-filled scene,
A comedic world where nothing's routine!

The Half-Light of Forgotten Paths

In the woods where whispers dwell,
Beneath the trees, the critters tell.
Squirrels wear hats, or so they claim,
While rabbits hop, all wild and tame.

Mice dance jigs on the old stone wall,
Singing songs of a grand old ball.
The foxes gossip in perfect glee,
Over acorns brewed in herbal tea.

Owls roll their eyes, so wise and keen,
As raccoons rave about their cuisine.
With every step, a giggle grows,
Among the leaves, the laughter flows.

So roam the paths where fun takes flight,
In the half-light of an endless night.
With fur and feathers, join the spree,
In this quirky forest jubilee!

Under the Watchful Branches

Beneath the canopy so wide,
The creatures gather, side by side.
A squirrel juggles, a fall and roll,
While a wise old owl keeps the scrolls.

Woodpeckers drum a raucous beat,
As hedgehogs compete in a tiny feat.
The beavers chortle, building their dams,
While badgers laugh in their little clams.

Frogs croak songs about the moon,
As fireflies dance in a merry swoon.
The branches sway, the laughter spins,
In a woodland world where fun begins.

Under these branches, all is bright,
With giggles echoing into the night.
So join the throng in this merry patch,
Where every creature has a match!

A Tapestry of Gnarled Secrets

In twisted limbs, tales are spun,
Of mischievous deeds under the sun.
The raccoon, dressed in striped attire,
Plays peek-a-boo, never to tire.

Gnarled roots weave a tale so grand,
Where pixies dance and rabbits band.
With every twist, the stories grow,
The forest whispers, shush, and flow.

The hedgehogs don their spiny hats,
Making friends with the chattering chats.
Mushrooms giggle in rainbow hues,
As the wind carries their playful news.

Each secret shared among the trees,
Brings giggles carried by the breeze.
In this tapestry of fun and cheer,
The heart of the forest draws us near!

The Quiet Heart of the Forest

In stillness found, a secret place,
Where trees wear smiles, each with grace.
The whispers giggle, bubbling clear,
While the flowers twirl without a fear.

A turtle races, oh what a sight!
Though slow in motion, he feels so light.
The ants parade in synchronized lines,
With tiny hats and their best designs.

Even the shadows crack a grin,
As the little critters pipe and spin.
Deer play hide and seek by the brook,
In this quiet heart, take a look.

Though tranquil art, the fun is near,
In nature's laugh, there's nothing to fear.
So join the peace, let joy impart,
In the quiet heart, of every heart!

The Play of Greys in the Forest

In the forest, greys do prance,
Squirrels dance a silly dance.
Leaves giggle, twirling round,
Nature's clowns in joy abound.

Mushrooms wear their hats so tall,
While chipmunks chase and trip, they fall.
A deer stumbles, gives a wink,
Even trees start to rethink.

Breezes tease with playful glee,
Tickling everyone, even me.
Wolves snicker from their dens,
Planning mischief time again!

Laughter echoes through the glade,
In this realm, the humor's laid.
Bright moon laughs with twinkling light,
Forest jesters through the night.

Flickering Fables of the Thicket

In the thicket, tales unfold,
Of creatures slightly bold.
Mice in capes and hats too wide,
Capering around with pride.

Owls with glasses, wise and sly,
Rolling eyes as frogs jump high.
A rabbit tells a joke so bad,
Even the pine trees feel sad.

Flickering lights from fireflies,
Join in for comic highs.
They glow as if to say,
'Let's laugh the night away!'

Every twig has laughter stored,
While nightingale takes on the chord.
In this thicket, joy ignites,
With every rustling of the lights.

Burdened Branches at Dusk

Branches droop with fruit so ripe,
Birds sit tight, ready to snipe.
Each nut crack holds a surprise,
As squirrels plead with puppy eyes.

Beneath the boughs, a raccoon lies,
Stuffed with snacks, he cannot rise.
His friends giggle, tease in fun,
Their antics prove a good day's done.

Glowbugs try to form a line,
To deliver news, oh so fine.
But tripping over roots and stones,
They make the sounds of old chattering phones.

At dusk, the branches sway and sway,
Carrying laughter into the fray.
For in their leaves, secrets weave,
Tales and giggles never leave.

The Calm Amidst Thorns

Here in thorns, a jest is found,
Bumblebees buzzing all around.
They sip from petals soft and sweet,
While prickles tickle little feet.

A hedgehog rolls in laughter's bliss,
Dodging thorns, not one he'll miss.
His friends chuckle, hearts so light,
As they tussle till it's night.

Thorns may guard, but joy stays near,
In every corner, laughter's cheer.
Flowers bloom in giggly rows,
Where humor quietly grows.

So in the thickets, don't you frown,
For laughter wears its prickly crown.
With beaming smiles through thorns and strife,
The calm brings forth the joy of life.

Streets of Silence and Solitude

In quirky lanes where silence strays,
A squirrel jokes in a nutty daze.
The benches giggle, lost in dreams,
As pigeons plot with clumsy schemes.

The lampposts lean, they whisper sly,
While mice in top hats waltz on by.
A dog in sunglasses barks a tune,
As cats rehearse their own cartoon.

The rain starts dancing, all aglow,
The puddles join in, putting on a show.
It's quite the party beneath the moon,
Where laughter lingers, ending too soon.

Through quirky streets where mirth prevails,
Every echo tells tall tales.
In solitude, the fun won't fade,
Adventure's waiting, unafraid.

The Cradle of Forgotten Voices

In a place where whispers dare not tread,
A ghost forgets the words once said.
Their giggles echo through the air,
As shadows find a slip of flair.

A jester's hat upon a tree,
Complains it's lonely, oh so free!
With hiccuping wind and rusting chime,
They snack on giggles, all in time.

Forgotten tales in the crook of night,
Perform for stars that twinkle bright.
Each chuckle held in a book of dreams,
Where laughter dances, or so it seems.

Echos paint the silence bold,
With colors bright and stories told.
In this cradle, every voice finds sound,
A merry shout, where joy is found.

Beneath the Cloak of Green Enchantment

Underneath the leafy veil,
A turtle spins a crazy tale.
The toads in tuxedos gather near,
To croak their anthem, quite sincere.

In the arms of starlit sprigs,
Dance the ants with tiny jigs.
A bumblebee with a booming laugh,
Conducts a band, oh what a gaffe!

Mushrooms sport their polka dots,
While fireflies offer dance floor spots.
Each rustle and giggle weaves the nights,
In enchanted laughter, pure delights.

So join the revels, light and free,
In the cloak of glee, can't you see?
The world is spun in joyous jest,
Where every creature lives their best.

Nestled Dreams Within the Woodlands.

In a grove where squirrels play,
Acorns launch in a wacky way.
Raccoons juggle nuts, so spry,
While owls hoot a comical cry.

Mice skate on leaves, full of glee,
Chasing each other, can't you see?
A tortoise tripped, oh what a sight,
He laughed it off, not a fright.

Trees wear hats of leafy green,
Dancing under the sun's bright sheen.
Bees wear ties, buzzing so bright,
It's a woodland party, pure delight.

Beneath the moon's silver light,
Frogs croon songs that'll bring delight.
Crickets dance with a wild swing,
Nature's comedy is in full swing.

Whispers Beneath the Canopy

Beneath the leaves, a rabbit pranced,
In a silly jig, he almost danced.
Squirrels chattered nonsensical news,
While chipmunks wore their fanciest shoes.

The shadows played hide and seek,
With critters chuckling, cheek to cheek.
A deer stumbled while trying to grin,
The forest echoed with laughter akin.

A raccoon made a big balloon,
Floating high, he aimed for the moon.
But the twig snapped, and down he came,
Landing right in a mud puddle game.

Whispers of giggles filled the air,
As foxes styled their fluffy hair.
Nature's jesters, all around,
In this funny realm, joy is found.

The Veil of Ancient Boughs

Under boughs where antics reign,
A squirrel slipped and caused a chain.
The branches shook with everyone's cheer,
As laughter echoed far and near.

A wise old owl, with glasses perched,
Spoke in riddles while the critters searched.
"Why did the spider cross the path?"
They chuckled and clutched their sides with wrath.

The whispering winds shared jokes untold,
As flowers giggled, colors bold.
The acorn fell with a thud so loud,
Gathering all beneath the crowd.

Fireflies sparkled in the night,
Guiding dance parties in sheer delight.
Each creature joined the merry parade,
In playful jest, no happiness delayed.

Echoes in the Twilight Grove

In twilight's glow, the fun begins,
Animals gather, let's see who wins.
A hedgehog spun, oh what a show,
While his friends cheered, "Go, go, go!"

The moonlight cast their funny grace,
As critters took turns in a wild race.
A turtle led, but you should know,
He was late; his brother stole the show.

The night was full of snickers and tales,
Where every critter has funny fails.
Raccoons wore socks upon their ears,
Embarrassed giggles filled the spheres.

Swaying branches joined the rhyme,
As whispers echoed in perfect time.
While laughter wrapped around each tree,
In this playful grove, all are free.

The Journey Within the Veils of Green

In the park where giggles bloom,
A squirrel wears a tiny broom.
Leaves whisper jokes to trees so grand,
While critters dance in a playful band.

Mystery lurks in every nook,
While rabbits plot a secret cook.
Unseen pals in the thickets peek,
With laughter flowing, oh so sleek.

A wise old owl with a twinkling gaze,
Tells tales of long-forgotten days.
Every twist and turn brings a smile,
Nature's humor, oh so versatile!

Follow paths of glowing cheer,
Where nature's pranks bring us near.
In the mist of laughter's sheen,
Life blooms bright in shades of green.

When Wood Meets Wonder

In the forest, a tale unfolds,
Of woodpeckers with dreams so bold.
They knock, they peck, in a rhythmic spree,
Creating laughter beneath the tree.

A bear with shades, lounges by the brook,
Reading a book, oh, what a look!
His toast by the fire—crunchy and brown,
He waves to the frogs as they jump up and down.

The trees hum songs of seasons past,
As the ginger cat climbs, moving fast.
With acorns and giggles, they cast a charm,
In a world so warm, they mean no harm.

Together they weave a tapestry bright,
Of wood and wonder, delighting in light.
In every leaf, a chuckle is found,
As laughter dances all around.

Canvas of Silhouettes

Under the moon, creatures play,
In a theater made of clay.
A raccoon dons a masquerade mask,
While friends gather, oh what a task!

Woodland shadows begin to prance,
In a clumsy yet graceful dance.
With twirls and spins, they steal the show,
As the fireflies blink, to and fro.

An owl hiccups, the audience roars,
As laughter echoes through the woods' doors.
Each brushstroke of night, a story to tell,
In silhouettes where all creatures dwell.

With every giggle, shadows come alive,
In this playful wood, they truly thrive.
So grab a seat in this echoing space,
And lose yourself in joy's warm embrace.

Embracing the Quiet Timbers

In the quiet timbers where laughter hides,
The chipmunks joyride on cedar slides.
A giggle here, a snicker there,
Every corner whispers a silly flair.

Foxes sport hats with a dapper tune,
Waltzing along a silver moon.
With old man tree cracking up in glee,
While the brook chuckles, "Come dance with me!"

In gentle winds, secrets are spun,
Of pinecone picnics under the sun.
From a thicket a voice calls, "What's the fuss?"
A porch of mushrooms, gather 'round us!

It's a party where silliness reigns so bright,
Embracing the quiet with sheer delight.
Nature's humor is a delight to find,
In the timbered realms where joy's entwined.

When Light Meets the Wood

In a glade where sunbeams play,
The squirrels leg wrestle all day.
A chipmunk sings a silly tune,
While owls roll eyes to the moon.

The laughter bounces off the bark,
As rabbits hop with a loud quark.
They trip on roots, then glide like pros,
Who knew nature had such funny bows?

In a dance of light and shade,
The sunbeams join the happy parade.
With giggles echoing in the breeze,
All nature's chuckling with such ease.

And down below, where shadows blend,
A raccoon tries to do a bend.
It tumbles over, rolls in glee,
A circus act for all to see.

Beneath the Canopy's Embrace

Underneath the leafy green,
A party forms, a lively scene.
With beetles sporting tiny hats,
And ants in lines, as choreo chats.

The sun peeks through, a cheeky tease,
As butterflies dance in the breeze.
A deer cracks jokes, oh what a sight,
While raccoons plot a midnight bite.

Fungi bounce like friendly clowns,
In colors bright, they wear their gowns.
With critters laughing all around,
They've really turned the woods to sound.

A gathering of timbered mirth,
Celebrating in earthen girth.
Where giggles spread from tree to tree,
In nature's jolly jubilee.

The Aged Sentinel's Promenade

An ancient tree, with wisdom vast,
Stands proudly as the world goes fast.
It wiggles branches, just for fun,
While birds parade, each wearing one.

Squirrels act as bellhops, you see,
With acorn hats, so fancy and free.
A lizard struts with a smug little tune,
Claiming it's also a woodland tycoon.

The leaves join in with a rustly cheer,
Saying, "Don't fret, we're all friends here!"
And as the sun sets on this grand stage,
The tree tells tales—oh, the wisdom of age!

With giggles shared 'neath the gnarled limbs,
Even the shadows play little whims.
For every step in this woodsy spree,
There's laughter hiding behind every tree.

Lament of the Twisted Trunk

Once a straight tree, proud and tall,
Now a twist, not caring at all.
It laughs at lines it no longer keeps,
As critters gather for woodland peeps.

The branches wave in quirky sprees,
While bees buzz by with jokes on the breeze.
It wobbles here, and leans on that,
Such antics fit for a silly chat!

A little raccoon hops on its back,
Claiming it's the head of the pack.
With every bounce, a story it tells,
Of cozy corners where laughter dwells.

Though its trunk is bent, its humor's straight,
Inviting all for a funny fate.
With every chuckle, it leans with pride,
In this crazy wood where giggles abide.

Where the Light Gets Lost

In the thicket where squirrels play,
Light trips over roots in dismay.
Jokes get tangled in branches rough,
While shadows giggle, never tough.

A raccoon winks, wearing a hat,
Saying, "Come join me, where's the mat?"
Laughter dances in the fallen leaves,
As the chatty voyeurs weave in eaves.

The sun whispers tales of the day,
But giggles bog down the sunny ray.
Each critter below tells their best quip,
Not a care as they spill from their lip.

In a land where the blunders grow tall,
And irony's king in the forest hall.
Where every breeze comes with a pun,
And even the mushrooms have too much fun.

The Dance of Leafy Sentinels

Beneath the canopy's sway and twirl,
Leaves shake hands; watch them whirl!
Gossiping lightly on the breeze,
Every vine winks, aiming to tease.

Swaying branches with shoes too big,
Crumble under the weight of a gig.
Moaning oaks spill tales of the past,
With snickers that rattle, unsurpassed.

The wind gets a kick from ticklish boughs,
Promising chuckles beneath their brows.
Each rustling paper from above,
Tells of mischief, laughter, and love.

In the heart of this leafy fun fest,
Even the quiet ones join the jest.
So come take a leap in this leafy swirl,
We'll dance till the night makes the stars unfurl.

Hushed Murmurs in the Grove

In whispers low, secrets unfold,
Sticks share tales both strange and bold.
The critters all lean in, very close,
To catch every giggle, the biggest dose.

Beneath the branches, laughter soap,
Plants pass notes, bubble, and grope.
"Did you hear what the old oak said?"
"Something about a barn and a sled?"

A hedgehog chuckles, ticks off a score,
While rabbits roll in giggles galore.
The toad croaks out, "Just listen in!"
As nature fills benches at whimsy's inn.

So gather 'round, for the night is sly,
Where each whisper decides to fly.
In a grove where the quiet looms wide,
The humour drips down with every tide.

Veils of Twilight in the Wood

As dusk wraps its cloak with a smile,
Creatures emerge, a curious file.
The fox cracks jokes with a sparkle in eye,
While owls tumble in a confused sigh.

The fireflies flash their brightest glee,
In antics that only they can decree.
There's a bard of the brambles crooning a tune,
While the whole forest giggles 'neath the moon.

Branches reach finely to catch the quirks,
While all the shy critters escape from their lurks.
Whispers of giggles float up to the stars,
As the night sprinkles joy in its jars.

With shadows now painted by night's colored brush,
And mischief afoot, the nocturnal rush.
Join in the laughter, it's time to rejoice,
For in the twilight, we all have a voice.

Branches that Embrace the Dusk

In the twirling breeze they dance,
Laughter ringing, give a chance.
Branches giggle, sway and twist,
Playing games that can't be missed.

As the sun begins to fade,
Furry critters start parade.
Squirrels don their tiny hats,
Dancing on the edge of chats.

Whispers float from leaf to leaf,
Sharing tales of stolen grief.
"Did you hear about that crow?"
He spilled his drink, what a show!

With each rustle, jesters play,
Mischief thrives at close of day.
Nature's circus, oh so grand,
Where all creatures lend a hand.

In the Realm of Swaying Shadows

In a corner of the park,
Where the light is faint and dark,
Frolicking with light and jest,
Creatures gather, feeling blessed.

Bunnies in their silly hats,
Prance around like acrobats.
With a quip, a bounce, a leap,
They dive into a pile heap.

Rabbits gossip, owls hoot loud,
Such a wild, wacky crowd!
Even trees begin to sway,
As they join the fun display.

Each shadow takes a turn to spin,
With a twist, let the fun begin!
Echoes of their laughter swell,
A tale that no one can quell.

Spirits of the Winding Trunks

In the forest, trunks converse,
With a grin, they joke and rehearse.
"Hey there, buddy, look at me!"
"I'm the oldest, can't you see?"

With mossy beards and bark so fine,
They share their tales over some wine.
But as they sip, a squirrel pounces,
Making all the wise ones bounces.

"Not in my house!" shouts the oak,
As all around bursts into smoke.
The laughter rings, the spirits cheer,
For mischief is their favorite beer!

With every knot and every twist,
New adventures they can't resist.
Side by side, they'll not grow old,
In their stories, life unfolds.

The Lament of Leafy Guardians

Up above, the leaves lament,
For crumbs of joy, they represent.
"Where is our friend, the playful breeze?"
"Gone for lunch, he has to tease!"

They swing and sway in grumpy tunes,
Wishing for those wobbly moons.
"Only flies come by these days,
With their buzzing, oh such craze!"

Yet just as they begin to pout,
A gentle gust gives a shout.
"Hey you grumps, let's cheer and play!"
"Join this dance, don't be so gray!"

With newfound joy, they twist and twirl,
Embracing every spin and whirl.
"Leaves of laughter, branch of fun!"
Together, under setting sun.

Echoes of Time Wrapped in Green

In a woodland where giggles play,
Time tiptoes in a leafy ballet,
Squirrels joke with acorns ripe,
While shadows dance in the moonlight hype.

A wise old owl wears glasses askew,
Cracking puns that make you go 'whoo!'
The tall trees chuckle, swaying tall,
As the sun slips down with a playful sprawl.

Hidden here are secrets sweet,
Of frolicking feet and a breezy beat,
Each rustle whispers a quirky tale,
Of a hedgehog who once tried to sail.

So join the antics, come and see,
Nature's circus, wild and free,
Where laughter weaves through each bright seam,
In this green domain, life's but a dream.

Limb and Leaf in Softest Embrace

Branches stretch in a joyful hug,
As leaves gossip like a cozy mug,
A chattering chipmunk spins a yarn,
While dandelions dance with a jaunty charm.

In this enclave, mischief is rife,
A bunny juggles, oh what a life!
The sun winks down through leafy masks,
While fungi tell tales, no one asks.

Tickled by breezes, laughter glints,
As bushes blush from their playful hints,
Caterpillars plot in a clever spree,
Sprouting butterfly dreams with glee.

Here in the green, the fun won't cease,
A carnival of whimsy, a flair of peace,
Where every twig's a chance to play,
In the warmth of a brightening day.

Enigmas of the Forgotten Grove

In secrets deep where whispers brew,
Beneath the branches, old and new,
A raccoon rehearses its stand-up set,
While the wind chuckles, won't forget.

Old stones gossip of days gone past,
While squirrels sneak in, dreaming fast,
A funny parade of the unseen,
Where frogs pose as kings, oh so keen.

Splintered logs hold hearty laughter,
In this grove of quirky after,
With tree roots plotting an epic race,
The path of giggles every place.

With every rustle and chirpy cheer,
It's clear this grove knows no fear,
For in its heart, where the wild things roam,
Laughter and joy find their home.

The Hiding Places of the Heart

Behind soft leaves, a treasure hides,
Where whimsy and wonder collide,
A small fox giggles with glee,
Playing hide and seek with a bumblebee.

In cozy nooks, the warm sun gleams,
As butterflies weave in dreamy beams,
An old tortoise tells jokes from his shell,
While tree branches sway with stories to tell.

Each burrow whispers secrets bright,
Where laughter sparks in the moonlit night,
The world is a stage, actors patrol,
In this lovely green, joy fills the soul.

So come, take a peek, find your delight,
In the hiding places of pure delight,
Where every tickle of grass will spark,
Fun-filled moments in the lark.

Specters of the Forest Floor

In the hush of the wood, they prance about,
Whispering secrets, with giggles no doubt.
Leaves tickle their feet, as they dance like fools,
Beneath the old trees, where nature drools.

A squirrel in glasses gives a wise old nod,
While ants cha-cha by, with a laugh and a prod.
Nutty debates hold the forest in thrall,
As fungi in hats join the jolly ball.

The moon peeks in, with a cheeky grin,
Watching the antics of creatures so thin.
Mushrooms look on, with a knowing glance,
While owls join in for a late-night dance.

At dawn they scatter, no evidence found,
Just the rustle of leaves and a fun little sound.
The laughter still lingers, like dew on a blade,
In this silly saga, no memory fades.

Enigma Wrapped in Leaves

A riddle of rustles, a puzzle of green,
Strange shapes in the thicket, what could they mean?
A hedgehog's top hat, a rabbit's ballet,
In a curious ballet, they frolic all day.

The whispers of ferns, all tied in a knot,
Each leaf holds a secret, a funny little plot.
Squirrels declare themselves kings of the jest,
A game of charades, they're simply the best.

The sun peeks through, with a mischievous beam,
Tickling the leaves, which giggle and scream.
The shadows may dance, but they cannot hide,
The humor afloat, like the breeze on a ride.

A riddle of laughter, a trail of delight,
In the twist of the woods, where the wrong feels so right.
With every odd glance, the enigma's complete,
Are we playing in circles, or just lost on our feet?

Sunlight's Foray into Darkness

Sunshine tiptoes, with a grin so wide,
Into the gloom, where shenanigans hide.
"Tag! You're it!" calls the cheeky old tree,
As laughter erupts from a family of bee.

The shadows giggle, they wiggle and sway,
As light beams perform in a very bright way.
Mischievous sprites sprinkle rays made of gold,
While mushrooms hold court, all huddled and bold.

A squirrel attempts a wobbly tightrope,
With acorns as weights, it's a slippery slope.
The sun can't stop chuckling, as it beams down low,
While shadows roll over, for the fun of the show.

A dance in the glade, where bright meets the gray,
With all of the forest, engaging in play.
Together they twirl, in a comical spin,
Where sunlight meets darkness, and laughter begins.

A Pilgrimage Through Pillars of Time

In a chapel of trees, where the old wood creaks,
Pilgrims of humor traverse with quirky tweaks.
With branches like arms and trunks like grand wands,
They whisper of days filled with silly fronds.

The owls consult maps, all covered in cheese,
While hedgehogs debate, as they giggle with ease.
"Which way to the fun?!" cries a mouse in a cape,
Underneath the great arch of a barky landscape.

Each step is a jest, every stride a surprise,
With fir trees high-fiving and giggling goodbyes.
The past greets the future, in a playful parade,
While laughter resounds, never to fade.

A pilgrimage once, now a party of joy,
In an ancient realm, they've found a new ploy.
Unraveling laughter in the fabric of time,
Where every twist and turn is brilliantly sublime.

Secrets of the Barked Behemoth

In the woods where the squirrels play,
A giant tree takes a snooze all day.
With branches like arms stretched wide and tall,
It snores so loud, it wakes them all.

The bees all buzz in a silly dance,
While ants wear hats and twirl in a trance.
Raccoons throw parties beneath its boughs,
Juggling acorns, they're quite the crowd.

Its bark is a canvas of stories untold,
Of silly mishaps from days of old.
A leaf whispers secrets in blissful glee,
"Dance with me, come climb this tree!"

When the moon peeks through with a cheeky grin,
The woods come alive with a raucous din.
From owls in tuxes to frogs in bow ties,
The night's a delight for all who surprise.

Dark Tresses of the Woodland

Underneath the branches so thick and lush,
The critters play in a wild, merry hush.
With hair like moss, the fairy hairdressers comb,
Each strand a secret; it feels like home.

A rabbit with ribbons hops to the beat,
While hedgehogs in shades dance on little feet.
The mushrooms provide a DJ in charge,
As the trees sway lightly, acting quite large.

With whispers of giggles in the cool shaded air,
A chorus of crickets sings without a care.
Behold the antics of the grand squirrel crew,
Trying on hats and shoes, oh what a view!

At dusk when the fireflies twinkle like stars,
The woodland boogies, without any bars.
With shadows that prance and creatures that jest,
The fun never ends, this forest's the best.

Mysteries Veiled in Green

In a grove where the rabbits wear monocles tight,
And hedgehogs debate what's wrong or right,
A tree with a grin shimmers with glee,
"Join me, my friends, come dance and see!"

The ferns hold secrets of nonsense profound,
Of whispers and laughter the woodland has found.
With jackets of ivy, the tree takes a bow,
And winks at the fox, "You're late! Oh, wow!"

An owl with a top hat, wise in his way,
Sips dew from a cup, watching squirrel ballet.
"Whooo's that dancing?" he hoots with delight,
As the party erupts with joy and goodnight.

So here in the green, where the kooky abide,
Adventures unfold with humor as guide.
Under the canopy where giggles break free,
Lies laughter and whimsy, a grand jubilee.

Dance of the Dappled Light

When sunlight pirouettes through branches and leaves,
And tickles the ground where all mischief weaves,
The woodland creatures don their best attire,
As shadows do jive around the campfire.

Squirrels strut proudly with acorn chic flair,
Dancing in pairs without any care.
The raccoons serve snacks, a splendid buffet,
With cupcakes and nuts to brighten the day.

Along twinkling paths where the daisies sway,
Bumblebees buzz in a groovy ballet.
Even the mushrooms have joined in the fun,
Twirling and spinning 'til day is done.

As night falls, the dancers sing out their tune,
With owls hooting softly at the bright moon.
In the dappled light, laughter echoes so bright,
The woods hold their secrets till the morning light.

Grove's Heartbeat in the Stillness

In the quiet nook of the woods so wide,
Squirrels hold a council, with nuts as their guide.
Trees bend low, whispering secrets and jest,
While mushrooms debate who's the most dressed.

The wind tries to play, but it slips on a twig,
And the brook giggles softly, in a water-swig.
Sunbeams cast patterns like playful pranksters,
Dancing on leaves like mischievous dancers.

Frogs in a chorus sing offbeat and loud,
While ants wear their hats, all proud and unbowed.
A badger, bemused, joins the scene with a grin,
Thinking he'd be quite dashing in a spin.

Oh, the wood's alive with a comical tune,
Where laughter and mischief are matched with the moon.
Each rustle and giggle a heartbeat of fun,
In the grove where the wilds know how to run!

Veiled Landscapes of Wonder

Behind every thicket, a riddle awaits,
A rabbit in glasses contemplates fates.
Wily old fox pretends to be wise,
While knickers and tails make the cleverest guise.

The hedgehogs play poker with acorns and twigs,
And all the owls hoot while doing a jig.
A raccoon dips low, yet thinks he's so sly,
Stealing a snack under the watchful sky.

Leaves wear their colors, all vibrant and spry,
As the sun plays magician, oh my, oh my!
With hats tipped to nature, the flowers all sway,
Dancing delight in a sprightly display.

In this hidden realm, where whimsy is king,
The laughter of branches starts tickling the spring.
Every critter a joker, a player at heart,
In these veiled landscapes, fun is the art!

Serenity Found in Knotted Roots

Under the gnarled limbs, the critters convene,
Telling tall tales of what might have been.
A tortoise in shades struts down the old path,
While the rabbits break out in a comedic laugh.

The roots intertwine like a dance of old socks,
As shadows play tag with their playful knocks.
A squirrel with flair tosses acorns in style,
While beetles tap dance all over the mile.

Mossy cushions cradle dreams of delight,
As the fireflies jive, twinkling so bright.
A gentle breeze teases the leaves, oh so spry,
In this corner of humor, where everyone's shy.

Serenity dances in the knotted embrace,
As laughter erupts in this green, cozy space.
In the quirkiest corners of nature's big room,
There's joy in the roots where the wild things bloom!

The Twilight Ballet of Branches

As the sun bows low, the branches all play,
In a twilight ballet where shadows can sway.
With whispers of mischief, the leaves come alive,
In a pirouette charm, they twist and they thrive.

A chipmunk in tails takes the lead with a spin,
While owls drop hints with a wink and a grin.
The branches applaud, with a rustle and cheer,
For every cute blunder, they hold oh so dear.

Bouncing beetles roll out a red carpet scene,
As crickets pick up their miming routine.
With frogs in the spotlight, singing off key,
The trees sway along, feeling wild and free.

In the dusk's perfect glow, the laughter takes flight,
As color and joy blend in magical light.
The ballet of branches, a comical show,
Where each star in the sky winks down to bestow!

Whispers Beneath the Canopy

Beneath the leaves, they chitter and chat,
A squirrel in a bow tie, how about that?
He spills the tea on the wise old owl,
With each witty quip, we can't help but howl.

The raccoons throw parties, wearing their masks,
They're champions of hide-and-seek, or so they ask.
While fireflies dance like tiny jazz bands,
Creating a tune that no one understands.

A hedgehog in glasses, reading his book,
Each page has a joke that'll make you go "ook!"
With laughter that ripples through night's tender air,
The midnight troupe knows naught of despair.

So let's join the fun, find our spot on the floor,
Under the branches where we laugh and explore.
In the giggles of critters, our worries take flight,
This forest of laughter makes everything bright!

Echoes of Weathered Bark

Listen close to the trees, they creak and they groan,
A woodpecker's knock sounds like a phone!
The sap runs sweet like gossip on a spree,
While branches exchange tales of the bumblebee.

An acorn dropped down, with a thud on the ground,
The squirrels are frantic, their treasure is found.
They plot and they scheme, oh the mischievous glee,
To stash all their snacks like a hoarding spree.

When the sun sets low, and the moon starts to rise,
The creatures convene, to their great surprise.
They argue not over who's best at the game,
But who serves the funniest story, and claim their fame.

The barks of the trees carry laughter around,
As critters unite with a jubilant sound.
In this circle of night, where the jokes are a lark,
Echoes of laughter dance through the park!

The Secrets the Night Holds

In the cloak of darkness, weirdness takes lead,
A cat wearing pajamas roams, yes indeed.
He's got tales to tell from his nightly pursuits,
Of mischievous mice wearing tiny black boots.

A wise old turtle rolls dice by a stream,
Predicting the weather, or so it would seem.
His friends in the reeds chuckle quietly,
Each guessing the outcome—what a sight to see!

Just around the bend comes a deer with a flair,
She taps her hooves gently, steals glances, and stares.
With a wink and a nod, she leads a ballet,
While frogs add the rhythm in their own silly way.

From fireflies buzzing to crickets that sing,
The secrets of night come—oh, what joy they bring!
In this whimsical world, we laugh till we fold,
As the moon whispers whimsies, and stories unfold.

Beneath the Twisting Limbs

Under branches bent like a funny old grin,
A badger in slippers invites us to spin.
"With pie on the table and jokes on the floor,
Let's dance till we drop, who could ask for more?"

There's a fox with a banjo, strumming away,
Telling tall tales with a twinkle of play.
His lyrics are silly, just nonsense and cheer,
But the way that he dances draws everyone near.

A family of owls, with their heads on a swivel,
Watch the commotion, give a low-hoot giggle.
They nod and they wink, enjoying the bliss,
For laughter is magic; it's simply their kiss.

So join in the revelry, clasp hands and twirl,
In this woodland escapade, feel joyous and whirl.
For beneath these twisted limbs, so alive with delight,
Are the secrets of laughter that sparkle at night!

www.ingramcontent.com/pod-product-compliance
Lightning Source LLC
Chambersburg PA
CBHW070750220426
43209CB00083B/255